⭐ FIVESTARMAN™

Field Guide
Manhood
GPS

Learning To Read God's Map

PJ McClure

Manhood GPS Field Guide: Learning To Read God's Map
ISBN 978-0-9829833-5-5

Editor: Linda A. Schantz

Cover Design: Peppermedia, LLC

Printed in the United States of America

Introduction

A field guide is generally used to showcase and explain the naturally occurring elements someone might encounter as they venture outside the classroom and into the actual environment of interest. This field guide for **Manhood GPS** is the same.

Broken up into daily topics, the contents of this guide will help you learn more about the parts of your GPS and how to navigate with it through life's twists and turns. Specifically, you will learn more about God, His attributes and how they apply to you.

As we discussed in the book, God is the world we live in. Our objective in life is to navigate within the framework of who He is. The more we understand, the better off we will be.

Each section of this guide has a focus, at least one scripture reference for a foundation, my commentary as it applies to your **Manhood GPS,** and a brief prayer asking for God's guidance to help you walk in the truth you have received. Some of the daily revelations are taken from stories of the heroes of faith in the Old Testament. Others contain rich spiritual principles presented in the Gospels and the letters written to the Early Church, and several are rooted in the multi-faceted truths found in the parables of Christ. As you read and meditate on the daily passages, ask the Holy Spirit to illuminate your mind and guide you into truth.

For additional study, in the back of this guide, there's also a listing of the references for many of the parables Jesus taught for you to study and draw out a deeper understanding of God's kingdom and His plans for your life. My hope is that you will actually open the Bible, read the referenced verses with their surrounding passages and spend a little time jotting down your thoughts on the lines provided for notes.

Remember: This book is not designed to let you vicariously experience God. Its purpose is simply to help guide as you adventure out on your own and build your own history with your Creator.

God speed and good adventuring!

Be your best,

— *PJ McClure*

DAY ONE

God is personal
and He wants to be known.

★ ★ ★ ★ ★

So He said, "I will certainly be with you."

Exodus 3:12a NKJV

It's possible that the idea of knowing God on a personal basis freaks you out a little. After all, how could He possibly want to be involved with someone as small, insignificant and faulty as you or I are?

There is a lie of the enemy that keeps us at a distance. "You're broken and unimportant. God doesn't want anything to do with you."

Yet, truth comes forward from the pages of Scripture to speak something totally different. God is interested. He reveals Himself in terms of relationship with man. In the person of Jesus, He took the entirety of our brokenness and carried it to the grave so we could have unimpeded access to His glory. Does that sound like someone who isn't interested?

Satan will do all he can to keep you in shame and hiding your face from your Heavenly Father, but God's purposes are far stronger than any lie. Start today to believe that He does know you, and He wants you to know Him.

PRAYER

Lord, thank You for loving me and wanting a close, personal relationship. I want to know You more. Reveal Yourself to me as I read the Bible and pray. Help me see You.

NOTES

_____
_____
_____
_____
_____
_____
_____
_____
_____
_____
_____
_____
_____
_____
_____
_____

DAY TWO

God is all powerful (omnipotent).

★ ★ ★ ★ ★

And what is the exceeding greatness of His power toward us who believe

Ephesians 1:19a NKJV

I can't count the times I've given up on something big just because I couldn't see how it was possible. It's really easy to get hung up on what we can't do and to forget that anything worth doing will be beyond our power any way.

The huge, impossible dreams God puts on our hearts are evidence of His love of adventure and the perfect opening for His glory. If we can do it without dependence on His mighty hand, there's no glory in it for Him.

Repeatedly during the Exodus account, God made it clear that He was orchestrating the miraculous deliverance of Israel in order to show Egypt and her neighboring nations, "I am Lord." God is still interested in showing the world that He is Lord! So what are you going after that provides an opportunity for that to happen?

Do you have the guts to go after something so big that the only way it can happen is if God directly intervenes? Will you and I continue in the face of seeming failure simply because we believe God Himself has ordained us to do it?

PRAYER

Lord, You are the mightiest! Nothing compares to Your power. I want the world to see Your greatness through my life. Please put a dream and plan in my heart so big it's impossible without You. Let everyone see how incredible You are through what you do in my life.

NOTES

_____

_____

_____

_____

_____

_____

_____

_____

_____

_____

_____

_____

_____

_____

DAY THREE

God is always with me (omnipresent).

★ ★ ★ ★ ★

Where can I go from Your Spirit? Or where can I flee from Your presence?

Psalm 139:7 NKJV

There are things I have done and places I have been to, of which I know God did not approve. When I used to talk about those times as part of my testimony I would call them, "times when I was far from God." That's only partially true.

The reality of life is that no one in this universe is ever far from God. Yes, our hearts and thoughts can be turned away from Him, but that's only *our part* of the equation.

God is always with us, regardless of whether we know it or not. In the depths of depravity, He is there, waiting and available if we decide to turn to him.

*...He is patient with you, not wanting anyone
to perish, but everyone to come to repentance.*

2 Peter 3:9 NIV

The Psalmist asked, *"Where can I flee?"* but the answer
is, you can't. Until you die, God pursues you. No matter
where you are or what you've done, He's right there, ready
to save you from yourself. All you have to do is ask.

PRAYER

*Jesus, I've felt so far from You at times in my
life, but I know that it was only because I
wasn't looking in Your direction. You have
always been with me and I've never been far
away. Thank You for walking with me. Now I
commit to walking with You.*

NOTES

_____
_____
_____
_____
_____
_____
_____
_____
_____
_____
_____
_____
_____
_____

DAY FOUR

God knows everything (omniscient).

★ ★ ★ ★ ★

If our hearts condemn us, we know that God is greater than our hearts, and he knows everything.

1 John 3:20 NIV

Life for us as mortal men is like the flow of a river. Everything moves in one direction and never stops. We dream of the future, which becomes the present and quickly turns into the past. Our ability to know anything is determined by our flow *to* and *through* the subject.

God, on the other hand, is outside the river and can see it all at once. He has no beginning or end. He sees everything as present. He knows our secret pain and true motives. Nothing is hidden from Him.

There is comfort in that knowledge for those who really want to live for and follow Jesus. I can have confidence when I go to Him with all my questions and concerns. But for those who are trying to get by on appearances only, that's a sobering revelation.

Our Lord's omniscience should comfort us. We know that nothing will escape His eye and we're always protected. But if it makes you uncomfortable to realize He knows all, perhaps it's time to truly turn your whole life over to Jesus.

PRAYER

Father God, I'm opening my entire life to You. Nothing is held back because I realize You see it all anyway. When I hold back I'm only separating myself from Your love and goodness, which are always for my benefit. Thank You that every part of my life is known to You and I don't have to worry about anything that might come against me as I live to serve You.

NOTES

_____

_____

_____

_____

_____

_____

_____

_____

_____

_____

_____

DAY FIVE

God is sovereign.

★ ★ ★ ★ ★

And all the inhabitants of the earth are accounted as nothing. And He does according to His will in the host of heaven and among the inhabitants of the earth, and none can stay His hand or say to Him, "What are You doing?"

Daniel 4:35 AMP

The concept of sovereignty is difficult for our modern sensibilities to grasp. It's a governmental word that has to do with total authority and control. In earthly terms, we see very little of it; however, when used in the context of the kingdom of God, sovereignty takes on its full meaning.

In a nutshell, saying, "God is sovereign," means that nothing happens that is outside His control. That doesn't mean He initiates everything, but it cannot happen unless He allows it. This creates many questions for us as finite creatures.

Why would a loving God allow some of the things we see to happen? I don't know for certain. What I do know is that He paints on a much bigger canvas than I can comprehend. What might seem like a mistaken brushstroke from my perspective may be the finishing accent to a beautiful masterpiece to Him. My job is to trust.

PRAYER

God, You are the glorious Creator and, as such, You are sovereign over all of Your creation. I believe You loved me enough to come and die for me and I believe that all the things I see happen in the world will eventually be used by You for good. Please give me eternal perspective so that the pains of this world do not keep me from living fully for You.

NOTES

_____

_____

_____

_____

_____

_____

_____

_____

_____

_____

DAY SIX

God controls time and seasons.

★ ★ ★ ★ ★

He changes times and seasons; he
deposes kings and raises up others.
He gives wisdom to the wise and
knowledge to the discerning.

Daniel 2:21 NIV

Growing up in southern Missouri I have always known the full four seasons... sometimes all in one week. Our Dutch immigrant neighbor once said, "Missouri is the only place you can scratch your sunburned back with your frostbitten fingertips."

As I have grown in the Lord it seems that life in the kingdom is similar, regarding the seasons of our lives. One season may seem to linger and slowly transition to another, but more often than not the changes are abrupt.

Our challenge is not to try to predict the length or change of seasons but to do the work we can in whatever season is upon us. Whether we are excited by the current season or not, we know God is working and we must look for our part in His work.

Spend less time wishing for a new season or for the current one to stay and more time asking for the strength to do what He's put in front of you.

PRAYER

Father God, I know You're in control of the natural seasons and the seasons of my life. I trust You to maintain or change the season I'm in according to Your glory. Thank You for giving me a role to play in Your plan, regardless of the season I may be in.

NOTES

_____

_____

_____

_____

_____

_____

_____

_____

_____

_____

_____

_____

_____

DAY SEVEN

God chose His people to become like Christ.

★ ★ ★ ★ ★

And we know that in all things God works for the good of those who love him, who have been called according to his purpose. For those God foreknew he also predestined to be conformed to the image of his Son, that he might be the firstborn among many brothers and sisters.

Romans 8:28-29 NIV

We're family, but not in the way most of us are used to. In God's family we're given the choice of inclusion. When we say yes to Him, we are born again, this time into the family of God.

A great distinction between our earthly and divine families is our individuality from our siblings. Parents go through great pains to encourage their children to "be themselves" and not to feel pressured to be like the older children in the home. Our Heavenly Father wants the opposite.

Our salvation is instant but the walk that follows is for life. Every twist and turn, good and bad, is a step toward us becoming like our oldest brother, Jesus.

The Father provided the Son, the Son provided the image, and the Holy Spirit helps us conform to that image. Our job is to realize this glorious truth and cooperate. See your circumstances as more than simple wins and losses. See them as the means to make you more like Jesus.

PRAYER

Jesus, thank You for the salvation You made possible on the cross and the amazing life You opened up to me through Your resurrection. I want to be like You in every way. I ask the Holy Spirit to work in all of my circumstances to help make this happen more each day.

NOTES

_____

_____

_____

_____

_____

_____

_____

_____

DAY EIGHT

God is generous
to all His children.

★ ★ ★ ★ ★

*The older brother became angry
and refused to go in. So his father
went out and pleaded with him.
"My son," the father said, "you are
always with me, and everything I
have is yours."*

Luke 15:28, 31 NIV

I have close friends who have lived more like the faithful
son in this parable than the Prodigal Son from which it is
named. One of the unfortunate side effects of such a life is
often having an inaccurate view of how God sees others who
have not lived so well.

Some who have been Christians for a long time have
developed an attitude that those who have sinned at higher
levels should somehow be treated differently — that they are
not eligible for the fullness of God's generosity.

Often this misbelief stems from another inaccurate picture of God. They think He doesn't want them to share in all He has. These people believe they must eek by on the minimum in life, as if being impoverished is the same as holiness.

But Jesus is clear that those who have lived faithfully have full access to the goodness of His kingdom and should be ready to celebrate in the same way when someone new enters, regardless of how they have lived before.

Our attitudes must reflect an accurate view of God as the generous and loving Father to all of His children or we will live below our station and resent those who live fully in His blessings.

PRAYER

Jesus, You are the perfect Son and, yet, You gave everything so I could also be a son of God. Please help me see others as You do and live in the fullness of sonship.

NOTES

_____

_____

_____

_____

_____

_____

_____

_____

_____

_____

_____

_____

DAY NINE

The Creator looks
after His creation.

★ ★ ★ ★ ★

*May the glory of the Lord endure
forever; may the Lord rejoice in
his works.*

Psalm 104:31 NIV

Go read the 104th Psalm right now. It will only take a couple of minutes, but the impact will be much more lasting.

We spend a lot of time wondering and complaining about the elements of nature and how they perform outside our control and convenience. Our uneasy relationship with supply and demand brings anxiety about our present state of affairs, and still we mouth the words, "God is in control."

Do we believe it? Do we act like we believe it? The way a good father is concerned for and looks over his family and their possessions, our Heavenly Father is infinitely concerned for and looks after His creation.

When we engage in complaining and worry regarding our own well being, we must answer a question about our focus. Is it on God or on us? If we are focused on Him, we're more willing to trust and operate in faith. If our focus is not on Him, we tend to create bigger messes for ourselves with our doubts and poor decisions.

The universe and all that is in it is under His watchful care. That doesn't mean He approves of all He sees or that He will interfere in the consequences of our actions. Will we trust His wisdom?

PRAYER

Lord, You care so much for Your creation and I'm so thankful to be part of it. I trust Your care for me and ask You to help me live each day and make every decision knowing You have a plan for my life.

NOTES

_____

_____

_____

_____

_____

_____

_____

_____

_____

_____

_____

_____

_____

Relationship with God requires worship.

★ ★ ★ ★ ★

Yet a time is coming and has now come when the true worshipers will worship the Father in the Spirit and in truth, for they are the kind of worshipers the Father seeks. God is spirit, and his worshipers must worship in the Spirit and in truth.

John 4:24 NIV

What does it mean to truly worship God? First, true worship can only come from a repentant, redeemed heart. Unless we are washed by the blood of Jesus, we can't even approach the throne to offer our worship. There is only one gate.

Second, our hearts must be fully turned to Jesus. Today, we may not offer our worship to physical idols the way the Samaritans of Jesus' day did, but there are many things in this world that can play for our affections. God must be our one, true desire.

Third, we must be in constant pursuit of God, and our every action should reflect it. How we handle business, compete in sports, treat women or distribute our finances tells the world what we desire most.

Worship is more than a style of music or a religious ritual. True worship is offering every bit of ourselves to God's glory and thanking Him for the opportunity to do so.

PRAYER

Dear Lord, I worship You. I turn my body, soul and spirit to You. To know and to love You are my true desires, and I live to show the world Your glory through my life. Please help me to give You worship in my songs, my actions and my thoughts so others can see Your love spreading throughout the world.

NOTES

_____

_____

_____

_____

_____

_____

_____

_____

_____

DAY ELEVEN

God is holy.

★ ★ ★ ★ ★

As obedient children, do not
conform to the evil desires you had
when you lived in ignorance. But
just as he who called you is holy,
so be holy in all you do; for it is
written: "Be holy, because I am
holy."

1 Peter 1:14-16 NIV

This may come as a shock, but you are not God and neither am I. So how is it that God Himself would inspire a command to be holy as He is holy? Yet another impossible act according to our own ability!

In navigating the kingdom of God we must remember that we're often given tasks and lifestyle demands that are purposely beyond our reach. By giving us these standards, God ensures our dependence on Him. He wants us close.

So if we are expected to do things we aren't capable of on our own, what part of the process is our responsibility?

Only the part within our control.

When I devote myself to God entirely I make decisions that reflect that devotion. I've walked away from my old, worldly ways. My thoughts and actions reflect purity. My worship is true and my service bears fruit that lasts.

We handle what is within our grasp for His glory and He, through scandalous grace, makes us holy and righteous children of God.

PRAYER

Thank You Jesus for removing the barrier between me and Your holiness. Because I have been placed in You by accepting Your salvation, I am holy in the eyes of the Father.

NOTES

_____

_____

_____

_____

_____

_____

_____

_____

_____

_____

DAY TWELVE

Don't put new wine in old wineskins.

★ ★ ★ ★ ★

And no one pours new wine into old wineskins. Otherwise, the new wine will burst the skins; the wine will run out and the wineskins will be ruined. No, new wine must be poured into new wineskins.

Luke 5:37-38 NIV

The Spirit of God is not meant to top off our existing life with a little refresher. When we accept Jesus as our Lord and Savior and receive His Holy Spirit, we are made new. All the past is forgiven, our old ways are dead and we are new vessels, ready to be filled with His righteousness.

In teaching the parable of the wineskins, Jesus let us know why this understanding is critical. If we think we can simply add on a little Jesus and everything will be okay, we've got another thing coming.

Trying to mix our old nature with the holiness Jesus provides will never work. The Holy Spirit will not cohabit with holdovers of sin. In order to truly receive and benefit from God's grace, love and wisdom, we must be fully new.

Look at your life right now and take a ruthless self-inventory. Are you a completely new vessel or are you trying to use Jesus to patch the broken places of an old life?

PRAYER

Jesus, I want to be a new wineskin and receive all the grace, love and wisdom You have for me. Holy Spirit, please help me see the holdouts from my old life — the impurities which will not mix with You. I commit to laying them down for Your glory in my life.

NOTES

DAY THIRTEEN

God imparts His holiness to believers through discipline.

★ ★ ★ ★ ★

They disciplined us for a little while as they thought best; but God disciplines us for our good, in order that we may share in his holiness.

Hebrews 12:10 NIV

Our society has a problem with authority and, by extension, with discipline. In an attempt to let everyone think they're right and to keep anyone from experiencing discomfort, we've lost the edge discipline brings.

The very root of discipline is the essence of life with Jesus. His followers were "disciples" or "those receiving discipline." When one or all of them made a mistake or revealed an incorrect thought about God, Jesus disciplined or corrected them so they could be ready to receive greater things.

Yes, sometimes discipline is uncomfortable or painful, and it is our attitude toward the one administering the discipline that determines our gain. If we're mistrustful of the person or their intentions, we're more likely to miss the lesson and growth.

When we fully trust God and realize His discipline is intended to allow us access to His holiness, we can trust the process and get the most out of our discipleship.

PRAYER

How amazing it is that You love me enough to guide me with Your loving discipline. I know there will be times I go astray and make mistakes, but knowing You will be there to bring me back into Your ways gives me confidence for all of the challenges ahead. You will not let me go.

NOTES

_____

_____

_____

_____

_____

_____

_____

_____

_____

_____

_____

_____

DAY FOURTEEN

God is absolute truth.

★ ★ ★ ★ ★

*To the Jews who had believed him,
Jesus said, "If you hold to my
teaching, you are really my
disciples. Then you will know the
truth, and the truth will set you
free."*

John 8:31-32 NIV

What is truth? What is actually right and wrong?

According to most of our society today, truth and right
and wrong are all relative to what feels good to you. In other
words, there isn't a moral standard by which to gauge
conduct.

These are lies.

What is more dangerous than the outright lies of moral relativity are the pastors and teachers who pick and choose what parts of the Bible they will believe and what parts they discard, as if God's Word is some sort of cafeteria plan

The validity of the Bible as we have it today has gone through more scrutiny than any other book in history. Guided from beginning to end by the Holy Spirit over thousands of years, it is the infallible and inerrant Word of God. To believe in only parts of it is one of the most ridiculous and arrogant acts of humanity.

We must decide if we believe or not. Every line is in agreement with every other line, and so it is completely whole. Believe and trust in one part, believe and trust in all of it... or don't. The decision is bigger than you may think.

PRAYER

Lord, thank You so much for Your Word! It is a lamp for my feet and a light for my path. I commit my life to Your truth and ask for more revelation as I study and meditate on the Holy Scriptures You have provided. I will hide Your words in my heart that I might always trust and follow You.

NOTES

_____

_____

_____

_____

_____

_____

_____

_____

DAY FIFTEEN

The Holy Spirit guides believers into all truth.

★ ★ ★ ★ ★

But when he, the Spirit of truth, comes, he will guide you into all the truth. He will not speak on his own; he will speak only what he hears, and he will tell you what is yet to come.

John 16:13 NIV

"He will guide you..." The Holy Spirit is the lynch pin of your **Manhood GPS**. In the way satellites orbiting Earth bring our natural GPS units to life, the Holy Spirit gives us an elevated perspective on our situation. But there's more!

Instead of just guiding us from one point to the next by reading the map of the land, the Holy Spirit guides us by telling us what the land wants us to know!

Since God Himself is the terrain we are navigating, His Holy Spirit connects us directly with the land under our feet. If we will set our hearts and minds to rely on His guidance and listen for His instruction, every stretch of our journey is divinely surrounded.

Just as Jesus was the direct connection and guide for those who physically walked with Him, the Holy Spirit is our connection and guide as we take our adventure.

PRAYER

I am so excited to know that I have the ultimate guide for my most important journey! Thank You Holy Spirit for revealing the mind of God and living inside me as I step into new and adventurous territory for Jesus. There are a lot of options calling for my attention in this world. I know You will guide me into all truth and tell me what's coming, so I can make the best decisions possible.

NOTES

_____

_____

_____

_____

_____

_____

_____

_____

_____

_____

_____

_____

DAY SIXTEEN

God is righteous.

★ ★ ★ ★ ★

You were taught, with regard to your former way of life, to put off your old self, which is being corrupted by its deceitful desires; to be made new in the attitude of your minds; and to put on the new self, created to be like God in true righteousness and holiness.

Ephesians 4:22-24 NIV

In Exodus 9:27 we are told God alone is righteous, yet Paul tells the Ephesians that our new self is created to be truly righteous. Impossible on the surface, but fortunately He gives us more to work with.

The old self, which is being taken off like old clothing, is corrupted by deceitful desires or the ways of this world.

Putting on the new self begins from the same place where the worldly desires used to live: our minds.

Just as he instructs in Romans 12, Paul tells us that our minds and thought life are where the real change begins. Our ability to approach righteousness and holiness comes from receiving and nurturing a new way to think.

Challenge yourself to think of righteousness as possible because you have been given a new self in Christ. Do not listen to the world's opinion of what you're capable of, but instead turn your thoughts, eyes and ears toward the One who makes all things possible for those who love Him.

PRAYER

Thank You Jesus for making me new! Please help me renew my thoughts and beliefs regarding my position in You. Reveal Your way of thinking to me and fill the spaces of my mind that were formerly held by the world with Your truth and love. I want to think like You.

NOTES

_____

_____

_____

_____

_____

_____

_____

_____

_____

DAY SEVENTEEN

God is just.

★ ★ ★ ★ ★

For we must all appear before the judgment seat of Christ, so that each of us may receive what is due us for the things done while in the body, whether good or bad.

2 Corinthians 5:10 NIV

"I want what's due to me!"

There's a constant lament about the entitlement mentality of the millennial generation. When you pay close attention to them it's hard to argue any other way. It seems we have an entire generation that showed up on the scene expecting to be given whatever they wanted.

Where do you suppose they learned it?

Entitlement is not a new concept, and at its roots it isn't bad. Similar to other fruits of liberty, however, it has been skewed and perverted to mean something that was never intended.

If we really received what we're due or have earned, the results would be different than most expect. Most of us want our due when we anticipate something good, but not so much when it's bad.

For those in Christ, we've already had the slate wiped clean. The death we deserved has been replaced with eternal life. We won't get what we deserve because of His mercy, but we're still building our case to stand at the Judgment seat of Christ. He will judge and reward justly, not with what we want, but with what we have earned in His service.

PRAYER

Jesus, thank You for saving me from the sinful death I deserved. I could have never earned salvation and You have provided it freely. Now help me to serve You with good works that will one day be rewarded according to Your goodness.

NOTES

_____

_____

_____

_____

_____

_____

_____

DAY EIGHTEEN

God is love.

★ ★ ★ ★ ★

*Who shall separate us from the
love of Christ? Shall trouble or
hardship or persecution or famine
or nakedness or danger or sword?*

Romans 8:35 NIV

We have a tendency to set conditions around everything. Since the definition of love has been reworked by society into something that's more of a feeling than a chosen action, we have attached conditions to it as well.

Early in the book of Romans, Paul reminded us that Jesus died for us while we were still sinners. In the garden before His death, Jesus was in anguish, sweating drops of blood, asking the Father if there was another way to accomplish our salvation. He obviously wasn't "feeling it."

Still, Jesus went on. He was and is unconditionally committed to our well being. That's the love nothing can separate us from. That's also the kind of love we're to show to others, especially our wives.

If you're married, are you showing unconditional love? Does your wife know nothing can separate her from your love? If you're single, are you prepared to be that kind of man?

Yes, love has feelings attached to it, and it can accurately be called an emotion, but feelings, or the lack thereof, do not determine whether love is present. Love is a choice. Love is a commitment. Love is an action, and Jesus removed the conditions.

PRAYER

Thank You Jesus for Your unconditional love! I want to love the way You love, and I need the Holy Spirit to show me how. Even in the times that are hardest to feel loving, please guide me in the truth of what love really is and how I can best show it to those around me.

NOTES

DAY NINETEEN

God corrects His children.

★ ★ ★ ★ ★

My son, do not despise the Lord's discipline, and do not resent his rebuke, because the Lord disciplines those he loves, as a father the son he delights in.

Proverbs 3:11-12 NIV

No man gets out of his car and yells at the guardrail after it prevented him from driving off a cliff. The rail is a safety measure that protects us from the worst-case scenarios of our own mistakes. We appreciate its presence.

Our attitude toward the Lord's guardrails should be the same. Because of His undying love for us, God puts up barriers intended to keep us from harm and to bring us back to Him. Barriers are a form of His discipline.

Yet we often get upset by these acts of God's love when they interfere with something we want to do but shouldn't, or worse, when the act is done and we knew the consequences ahead of time. Then when the discipline shows up, we act as if God has been unfair.

His willingness to keep us safe is born from the same father-heart He placed inside us — the heart that realizes, sometimes we must be confronted and made uncomfortable to learn what is best.

Remember that God loves and delights in you, and learn to appreciate His guardrails.

PRAYER

Lord, You are my shepherd. I trust You to keep me safe as I walk with You. When I wander away from Your side, I love that You bring me back. I know that Your rod of correction keeps me close and gives me comfort.

NOTES

DAY TWENTY
God is merciful.

★ ★ ★ ★ ★

*If we confess our sins, he is
faithful and just and will forgive
us our sins and purify us from all
unrighteousness.*

1 John 1:9 NIV

Sin is not based on opinions or degrees of guilt. No one is
made righteous because they agree with whether or not
something is sinful or by behaving better than someone else.
Our sin problem is handled one-on-one with the Savior of all
Creation.

Part of our salvation process is the confession of our sins
and the acknowledgment of Jesus as our Lord. The moment
we do this, we are forgiven, and our old nature, the one bent
toward the evil of the world, is taken away.

Even as born-again believers, we still commit sins, though, no longer as a lifestyle. When those times happen, we're still called to confess our sins and to ask for forgiveness. Praise God that He is faithful to forgive us each and every time!

God's faithfulness isn't a license for us to continue living the way we used to, but it does remove the shame the enemy would like us to carry around. If we will drop the false pride and humble ourselves to confess our sins and accept His forgiveness, there's nothing that will keep us from God's presence.

PRAYER

Jesus, You made a way for me when there was no way. Because of You, I can boldly come before the throne of grace and know You will make me pure and righteous. I live confidently because of Your grace, and others are drawn to You because of my example.

NOTES

DAY TWENTY-ONE

Shed the shame.

★ ★ ★ ★ ★

...There was a man who had two sons. The younger one said to his father, "Father, give me my share of the estate." So he divided his property between them. Not long after that, the younger son got together all he had, set off for a distant country and there squandered his wealth in wild living.

Luke 15:11-13 NIV

If we allow ourselves to be honest, the parable of The Prodigal Son is relatable to our experiences prior to salvation.

We start out with every spiritual advantage in life because God already loves us with an undying love. But we approach His love with a sense of entitlement and waste it on satisfying our selfish, temporal desires. Only when we've hit rock bottom do most of us come to our senses.

The enemy applies his most common lie at the point of our revelation. We realize the magnitude of our sin and a demon whispers in our ears to tell us how shameful we should be, that God would never want to be close to someone so wretched.

Truth tells us just the opposite. God is a loving Father who is always ready and waiting with great anticipation for His wayward children to come home so He can restore them to the fullness of His family.

No matter what you've done, shed the shame and receive His forgiveness. Your Father is waiting for you.

PRAYER

Father God, I repent for being so reckless and selfish with Your love. Thank You for making it possible for me to come back to You. Thank You for welcoming me home.

NOTES

_____

_____

_____

_____

_____

_____

_____

_____

_____

DAY TWENTY-TWO

God is faithful.

★ ★ ★ ★ ★

No temptation has overtaken you except what is common to mankind. And God is faithful; he will not let you be tempted beyond what you can bear. But when you are tempted, he will also provide a way out so that you can endure it.

1 Corinthians 10:13 NIV

I hear a lot of people giving God the blame for the things the devil is behind. Temptation is not God's doing, but it does fall within His jurisdiction to act upon the situation.

Idolatry, sexual immorality and many other forms of worldly temptation surrounded the people of Corinth. Undoubtedly, after their conversion, they were tempted to satisfy some of the same fleshly desires they indulged in before coming to Christ. They may have wondered why God would allow them to continue to be tempted by such things.

Our world is similar to theirs, and our temptations are too. Fortunately, the same glorious truth written to the Corinthian believers applies to us. When the enemy of our souls puts a temptation in our way, God does not turn His head.

Instead, God puts a boundary on the temptation and creates an escape for us! If we will simply look for His truth and make decisions based on what we know about pleasing God, the tempter cannot win.

When the odds seem stacked against you and an old temptation comes calling, trust God to keep His promises.

PRAYER

I could never navigate this sinful world without You, Lord. Thank You for always providing a way out of temptations and helping me to grow stronger in endurance at the same time.

NOTES

_____

_____

_____

_____

_____

_____

_____

_____

_____

DAY TWENTY-THREE

God never changes.

★ ★ ★ ★ ★

*I the Lord do not change. So you,
the descendants of Jacob, are not
destroyed.*

Malachi 3:6 NIV

The descendants of Jacob were the children of
tremendous promise. From the days of their forefather
Abraham, God had given unprecedented promises to the
entire family, which had become a large nation.

By the time the prophet Malachi came onto the scene, the
nation of Israel had lived in cycles of blessing and of poverty
due to their inability to maintain a right relationship with
God. By all measures, they had forfeited their rights to the
promises by their own misdeeds against the Lord.

But through the prophet, God reminded the people of
their greatest hope: Him. "I do not change," He told them.

Meaning, the promises He made generations before were still in effect. Those promises were the reason they had not been wiped off the face of the earth.

We, by adoption, are also descendants of Jacob. We have access to and are protected by those same promises.

Our moods and motivations may change for little or no reason, but not our God. He is the Rock, the only unshakeable foundation we can build our lives upon. The unchangeable God of ancient Israel is the God of our today.

PRAYER

Praise You, God, for being my Rock! This world is always shifting and moving, but You are the same for all time. I give You praise and honor as I build my life upon You.

NOTES

_____

_____

_____

_____

_____

_____

_____

_____

_____

_____

_____

_____

_____

_____

DAY TWENTY-FOUR

Be faithful with
what you have.

★ ★ ★ ★ ★

*To one he gave five bags of gold,
to another two bags, and to
another one bag, each according to
his ability....*

Matthew 25:15 NIV

Comparison with those around us is one of the most dangerous traps in life. If we aren't careful, our decisions become detours to try to make us similar to or better than someone else, instead of tools to help us be our best.

I've often wondered how it could be part of God's will that some people would be born into advantageous situations and others into seeming disadvantage. Those with the obstacles in their paths could never be expected to achieve the same results as those who start so far ahead.

In the parable of the talents, Jesus shows us how God views such circumstances. All three of the servants in the story were given different starting points, *"each according to his ability."* The master knew the capabilities of each servant and entrusted him with what he felt they could handle.

Though we aren't told, it is possible that the five-bag man started off as a one-bag guy who proved he could handle responsibility. If so, each time he proved faithful with what was entrusted to him, his ability would have increased. In turn, each time his ability increased, the master could give him more to handle.

Do not despise small beginnings. Be faithful with what you have and where you are now and your ability will grow.

PRAYER

Father God, thank You for trusting me. I know that as I prove faithful with the small things, You will increase my responsibility and blessings.

NOTES

_____

_____

_____

_____

_____

_____

_____

_____

_____

_____

DAY TWENTY-FIVE

God's words create and sustain everything.

★ ★ ★ ★ ★

The Son is the radiance of God's glory and the exact representation of his being, sustaining all things by his powerful word.

Hebrews 1:3a NIV

The words of God are the most powerful force in existence. With His words, all things were created, and those same words sustain all Creation.

Jesus Himself is repeatedly called "The Word," indicating the position of importance given to words in the kingdom of God. There's an element of this we must grasp as men in order to fulfill our potential impact in God's plan.

We are created in the image of God and therefore have a measure of His creative power in our words. No, we can't speak a new universe into being, but we can create the environment our family lives in.

Each word from our mouths has the ability to build or destroy — to give life or to take it. Until we take full responsibility for our words and use them with the level of intention they deserve, we will live an inferior life, bringing those around us down too.

Make it a point to bridle your tongue and make it go where you want. Left unchecked, your words will create nothing but broken pieces in your life to pick up and try to put back together. Instead, be a builder of health and faith.

PRAYER

Dear Lord, through Your words everything came to be, including me. I can hardly get my head around how You gave me a measure of Your creative power by giving me the ability to speak words of life. Help me build others up with my words each day as You intended.

NOTES

_____

_____

_____

_____

_____

_____

_____

_____

_____

_____

God is the powerful Deliverer.

★ ★ ★ ★ ★

In days to come, when your son asks you, "What does this mean?" say to him, "With a mighty hand the Lord brought us out of Egypt, out of the land of slavery."

Exodus 13:14 NIV

Throughout history men have found themselves enslaved by some brutal taskmasters.

For ancient Israel, the same Egyptian nation that was saved from ruin by God's work through Joseph was now oppressing the Israelites because of new leadership. Though mighty in number, Israel was not able to free themselves from the bonds of slavery.

Realizing their helplessness, Israel cried out to God for deliverance and set the Exodus in motion with a series of signs and wonders that only He could accomplish. Faithful to His Word, God delivered Israel.

Today we see men enslaved by their own choices in everything from their pursuit of money to sexual immorality. These taskmasters are just as brutal and unyielding as the Egyptian Pharaoh.

But God is just as faithful now to deliver us from these bonds as He was to deliver Israel.

What is holding you captive? Cry out to God and ask for deliverance! He will free you with His power!

PRAYER

Oh God, my mighty Deliverer! Set me free from these chains! I will follow Your every command and will keep a memorial of Your deliverance in order to tell others the reason for my hope and to draw them closer to You.

NOTES

_____

_____

_____

_____

_____

_____

_____

_____

_____

_____

_____

God's continual presence brings contentment.

★ ★ ★ ★ ★

Be strong and courageous. Do not be afraid or terrified because of them, for the Lord your God goes with you; he will never leave you nor forsake you.

Deuteronomy 31:6 NIV

When Moses was departing the scene and Joshua was taking over as leader of the nation of Israel, they had one of the best succession plans ever.

Joshua served as aid to Moses from the time they left Egypt, and Joshua had the best seat in the house to witness the face-to-face relationship God had with Moses. What I love about Joshua's story more than that, though, is how many times God said to Joshua, "I will be with you."

This grips me, not because of God's willingness to be with Joshua, but because of Joshua's track record of not leaving God. We see the first indication of Joshua's devotion when he would not leave the Tent of Meeting after Moses had left (Exodus 33).

I believe Joshua knew the deep sense of contentment we experience in the Lord's presence and Joshua wanted to be with God always. Our advantage over Joshua is that God's presence on Earth dwells within us, not in a tent or church. We can always stay in His presence because His presence is within us!

PRAYER

Lord, I'm blown away by realizing that I can always be in Your presence! I know the only contentment to be found in this life is found when I focus on being present with You. When I lose that focus, please remind me to come back to You.

NOTES

_____

_____

_____

_____

_____

_____

_____

_____

_____

_____

Supressing God's truth can be perilous.

★ ★ ★ ★ ★

The wrath of God is being revealed from heaven against all the godlessness and wickedness of people, who suppress the truth by their wickedness.

Romans 1:18 NIV

Even though Paul wrote his letter to the church in Rome during the first century, he could have easily written it today. The same level of wickedness and perversion facing the Romans is present in full force in our society.

Massive political agendas are leveraged against the truth of God's Word. Influenced by the demonic, and driven by their own selfish desires, countless people align their resources to twist, distort and cover up the clearly expressed standards of our Lord.

Firestorm topics like abortion, homosexuality, marriage and more are bombarded constantly. Even some preachers, who have taken on the solemn and weighty role of shepherding God's people, are degrading the Bible in order to promote more socially acceptable ideals at their own peril.

They know the truth and have decided to align with the world instead. Jesus told us in John 15 that the world would hate us because we love Him. This is not a new idea, but it is a sobering warning.

As men, we must stand firm in the truths revealed in the Bible and be willing to sacrifice our popularity with others for the glory of our God.

PRAYER

Jesus, help me to discern attacks against Your truth and give me the words and actions to oppose the powers and principalities that would see Your truth suppressed.

NOTES

_____

_____

_____

_____

_____

_____

_____

_____

_____

_____

_____

DAY TWENTY-NINE

Jesus paid our debt.

★ ★ ★ ★ ★

*"Two people owed money to a
certain moneylender. One owed
him five hundred denarii, and the
other fifty. Neither of them had the
money to pay him back, so he
forgave the debts of both. Now
which of them will love him
more?"*

*Simon replied, "I suppose the one
who had the bigger debt forgiven."*

*"You have judged correctly," Jesus
said.*

Luke 7:41-43 NIV

When I fully came to my senses and realized the depth of forgiveness given to me by Jesus and His sacrifice, I began to let my praise and worship loose!

He rescued me from decades of huge mistakes and set me on level footing with Himself, in the throne room of Heaven, at the right hand of the Father. Wow! How else could I respond but with loud, joyous and exuberant praise?!

Still, those who had grown up in a more righteous way seemed to think I was a little over the top — as if my level of praise and thanksgiving was somehow undignified.

Jesus gives us a clear picture of how this can happen. Yes, we've all sinned, but only those who grasp the magnitude of their impossible debt will ever really worship God with everything they have. I was like the debtor forgiven the five hundred. How about you?

PRAYER

Jesus, please help me to grasp the magnitude of the debt You paid on my behalf. I want to love You with an unending, unrestrained exuberance in my body, soul and spirit!

NOTES

_____

_____

_____

_____

_____

_____

_____

_____

DAY THIRTY

Count the cost.

★ ★ ★ ★ ★

Suppose one of you wants to build a tower. Won't you first sit down and estimate the cost to see if you have enough money to complete it? In the same way, those of you who do not give up everything you have cannot be my disciples.

Luke 14:28, 33 NIV

Every endeavor of significance requires planning. Even the camping, floating or hiking trips my son and I go on frequently require us to make sure we have what we need to make the trips successful. It's foolish to begin without first considering what is required of us.

Jesus wants us to know that following Him is the most significant adventure we will ever take.

What will it require? What is the cost of the journey? Everything.

Nothing can have priority over Jesus. Just as when God commanded the Israelites to have no other gods or idols before Him, Jesus makes it clear that He will not accept half-hearted or weak commitments. He wants all of us.

Regardless of how easy we often make it seem when calling people to the altar, following Jesus is anything but easy. It requires the ultimate commitment of putting Him first in everything and allowing the rest to fall into place as a result.

Counting the cost of following Jesus isn't easy, but it is simple. Simply give Him everything.

PRAYER

Jesus, I have counted the cost and I give my entire life to You. I can't do it on my own, but know that the Holy Spirit will empower me to live completely for You.

NOTES

_____

_____

_____

_____

_____

_____

_____

_____

_____

_____

Our Father wants us to be with Him.

★ ★ ★ ★ ★

But while he was still a long way off, his father saw him and was filled with compassion for him; he ran to his son, threw his arms around him and kissed him.

Luke 15:20b NIV

Maybe you've squandered the amazing life given to you. Perhaps you've allowed circumstances to cloud your view of God's generosity and goodness. Regardless of how you've turned away from your loving Father, He's waiting with unbridled anticipation for you to return.

The parable of The Prodigal Son is most often used to talk about the Prodigal himself and how we can relate to his behavior, but the story is really about the father. Just like so many other parables He told, Jesus wanted us to see a picture of our Heavenly Father and to realize how desperately He wants us to be with Him.

We need to make note of this, the father in the story allowed his child to make a poor decision, but when the child came back, the father was ready to make everything right! Not only did he run to embrace his child, he restored him to full sonship by bestowing the symbols of the family upon him.

Our Heavenly Father is ever watchful for the return of His children. Our job, once we've returned, is to tell as many others as we can that the Father is ready to welcome and restore them as well.

PRAYER

Thank You, Father, for always loving and never giving up on me. By dressing me in Your Holy Spirit, I now show the signs of being in Your family. Help me to draw others to You by walking as Your son.

NOTES

_____

_____

_____

_____

_____

_____

_____

_____

_____

_____

Conclusion

THE JOURNEY CONTINUES

I trust these short excerpts from the Bible have shed some light on God's character and helped you get to know Him better; however, the depth and richness available through each of these references cannot be explored in one or two reads.

This is merely a starting point — a trailhead if you will — to a much larger journey. We will have all eternity to study and learn more about God and still never reach the end. I encourage you to go back to the parables of Jesus and pray for continued revelation as you study them.

To help, at the end of this field guide I've included a list of many of the parables of Jesus and where they are found. Each one provides keen insights and thought-provoking questions. Dive in and see what the Holy Spirit will reveal to you!

I always love to hear your stories of exploration and any questions you discover along the way. Come share what you've discovered and ask your questions on my blog, Facebook or Twitter.

Yours in the journey!

— PJ McClure

THE PARABLES OF JESUS

The Growing Seed	Mark 4:26-29
The Two Debtors	Luke 7:41-43
The Lamp Under a Bushel	Matthew 5:14-15, Mark 4:21-25, Luke 8:16-18
The Good Samaritan	Luke 10:25-37
The Friend at Night	Luke 11:5-8
The Rich Fool	Luke 12:16-21
The Wise and the Foolish Builders	Matthew 7:24-27, Luke 6:46-49
New Wine into Old Wineskins	Matthew 9:17, Mark 2:22, Luke 5:37-39
The Strong Man	Matthew 12:29, Mark 3:27, Luke 11:21-22
The Sower	Matthew 13:3-9, Mark 4:3-9, Luke 8:5-8
The Tares	Matthew 13:24-30
The Barren Fig Tree	Luke 13:6-9
The Mustard Seed	Matthew 13:31-32, Mark 4:30-32, Luke 13:18-19
The Leaven	Matthew 13:33, Luke 13:20-21
The Hidden Treasure	Matthew 13:44
The Pearl	Matthew 13:45-46
Drawing in the Net	Matthew 13:47-50
Counting the Cost	Luke 14:28-33

THE PARABLES OF JESUS

The Lost Sheep or Good Shepherd	Matthew 18:10-14, Luke 15:4-7
The Unforgiving Servant	Matthew 18:23-35
The Lost Coin	Luke 15:8-10
The Prodigal Son	Luke 15:11-32
The Unjust Steward	Luke 16:1-13
The Rich Man and Lazarus	Luke 16:19-31
The Master and Servant	Luke 17:7-10
The Unjust Judge	Luke 18:1-8
The Pharisee and the Publican	Luke 18:10-14
The Workers in the Vineyard	Matthew 20:1-16
The Two Sons	Matthew 21:28-32
The Wicked Tenants	Matthew 21:33-41, Mark 12:1-9, Luke 20:9-16
The Great Banquet	Matthew 22:1-14, Luke 14:15-24
The Budding Fig Tree	Matt 24:32-35, Mark 13:28-31, Luke 21:29-33
The Faithful Servant	Matt 24:42-51, Mark 13:34-37, Luke 12:35-48
The Ten Virgins	Matthew 25:1-13
The Talents or Minas	Matthew 25:14-30, Luke 19:12-27
The Sheep and the Goats	Matthew 25:31-46
The Wedding Feast	Luke 14:7-14

NOTES

NOTES

NOTES

About the Author

PJ McCLURE

PJ McClure is a rising voice in the movement to resurrect authentic manhood. As a mentor to young and older men alike, PJ communicates kingdom principles through writing and speaking to businesses, churches and schools.

He is a servant of Jesus, husband, father, pastor and endorsed communicator for *FivestarMan.*

Contact Information

For more resources or to schedule PJ McClure for
your church, business, conference or a personal consultation

PLEASE CONTACT:

PJ McClure
The Mindset Maven, LLC
4248 Hwy 83
Bolivar, MO 65613
PJMcClure.com

FOLLOW PJ:

Blog: *PJMcClure.com*
Facebook: *PJMcClurebiz*
Twitter: *PJMcClure*

www.ingramcontent.com/pod-product-compliance
Lightning Source LLC
Chambersburg PA
CBHW070758050426
42452CB00012B/2396